BLUES PIANO A-Z
A BEGINNER'S GUIDE TO BLUES STYLE, THEORY, AND IMPROV

By Jeremy Siskind

ISBN 978-1-70513-178-7

Visit Hal Leonard Online at
www.halleonard.com

Contact us:
Hal Leonard
7777 West Bluemound Road
Milwaukee, WI 53213
Email: info@halleonard.com

In Europe, contact:
Hal Leonard Europe Limited
42 Wigmore Street
Marylebone, London, W1U 2RN
Email: info@halleonardeurope.com

In Australia, contact:
Hal Leonard Australia Pty. Ltd.
4 Lentara Court
Cheltenham, Victoria, 3192 Australia
Email: info@halleonard.com.au

PRELUDE

For many musicians, learning the blues can be like learning their ABCs. Because it's accessible, expressive, and fun, the blues is the perfect place for a pianist to first encounter jazz and popular music. With experience and practice, however, pianists can transform those simple ABCs into poetry of the highest order. In fact, as a musician grows, their understanding of both the depth and breadth possible in the blues should grow boundlessly with them.

The pieces in this book are intended to guide a pianist from their very first encounters with the blues all the way to complex and sophisticated approaches to the style. My goal is that studying each piece will deepen the understanding and appreciation of the blues tradition.

Beyond the 26 pieces that span diverse levels and styles, 10 guided improvisation exercises are peppered throughout the book, each based on a through-composed piece. Since the blues is ultimately both deeply personal and deeply expressive, experiencing improvisation is integral to a deep understanding of the blues style. Please approach the improvisation exercises with the same seriousness and dedication as the written-out pieces.

A word about key signatures: Although some musicians identify blues forms as being "major" or "minor," the blues doesn't fit neatly into these Western categories. I've had long discussions and debates with musicians of all stripes about the most appropriate key signatures for the blues form, and the general consensus is that the composer has a lot of latitude to decide the best key signature. Therefore, I've decided on the key signatures that I think make the music easiest to read, in many cases omitting key signatures all together. Although these key signatures, or lack thereof, might seem strange to a classically trained musician, I invite you to embrace this different tradition.

The blues tradition is an oral tradition. For that reason, the text of this book frequently mentions artists who have made significant contributions in the history of the blues. To have the most authentic possible experience with the blues, listen to recordings of these artists, paying special attention to their style. Use what you hear to inform the way that you interpret these pieces and improvise.

The blues can be a stunning vehicle for joy and an eloquent way to cope with heartache. I'm wishing you fulfillment in your journey with this beautiful art form.

CONTENTS

The 12-Bar Blues

The **blues** is a chord progression with roots in the African American folk tradition. Because the blues chord progression is 12 measures long, it's sometimes called **the 12-bar blues**. As you're playing each piece, keep track of the 12-measure sections. Blues musicians call once through the blues progression a **chorus**. Throughout this book, you will find either double barlines or repeat signs at the beginning and end of each 12-measure blues form.

Blues forms are often extended by adding **introductions**, short passages intended to set the mood of the piece, and **endings**, short passages intended to bring the piece to a satisfying close. The most common ending for a blues is a **tag**, a device in which the last measure or two is repeated multiple times, allowing the piece to wind down gradually. If you see a blues form that appears to be more than 12 measures, it probably includes an introduction or ending.

The 12-bar blues progression is used by all kinds of musicians from rock guitarists to jazz saxophonists to R&B singers. Although the blues is usually associated with sadness, lots of musicians use the blues as a way to lift people out of their sadness and into joy. For example, James Brown's famous song, "I Feel Good," uses a blues progression for its refrain.

Play "All-American Blues" at a few different tempos to notice the change of mood. If you play it slowly, it might sound sad and mournful. But if you play it fast, you could start a joyful dance party! The blues has the remarkable ability to convey both profound sadness and profound joy.

All-American Blues

Jeremy Siskind

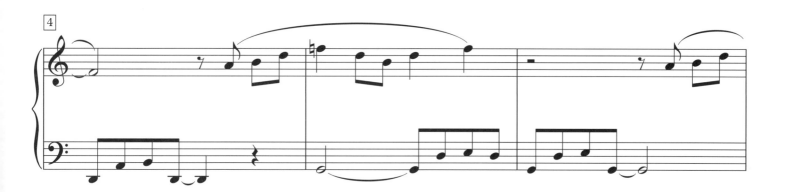

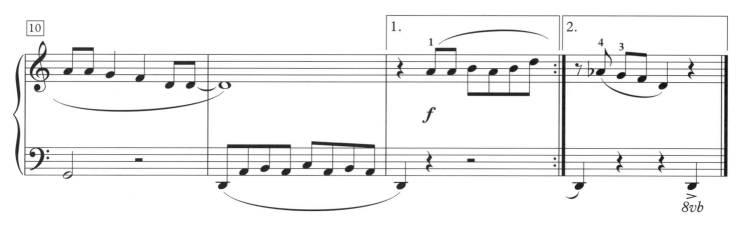

Call and Response

Call and response is a musical concept in which two instruments – or, in our case, two hands on the piano – "talk" to each other, trading phrases, one after the other. First, one hand plays a phrase while the other holds or rests. Then, the other hand takes the lead and plays a response phrase while the original hand holds or rests.

The two phrases in a call-and-response pattern should sound like a **question** and an **answer**. If you think about it, answers often repeat a lot of the words of a question. For example, if I ask you, "What songs do you like to play on the piano?", you might start by saying, "The songs I like to play on the piano are..." Questions and answers are highly repetitive in music too. As you play "Back and Forth Blues," notice that the answer phrases in the left hand often repeat material from the question phrases in the right hand.

Back and Forth Blues

Jeremy Siskind

Driving Rock (♩ = 136) *Both hands 8va on repeat*

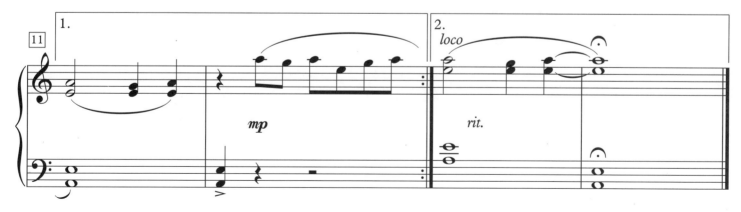

New Orleans

One place you might hear the blues is in **New Orleans, Louisiana**. The city is famous for its colorful street parades led by marching musicians. Here's a call-and-response tune in the New Orleans style. Imagine that you're standing on Canal Street, near the French Quarter, and you hear a trombone playing the left-hand question and a trumpet responding with the right-hand answer.

Canal Street Parade

Jeremy Siskind

Improvisation

Improvisation is the art of making up music on the spot. Just as we can hold a spontaneous conversation with words, improvising musicians can have spontaneous musical conversations. Improvisation is a core element of the blues tradition.

The notation to indicate that a musician should improvise is a series of **slashes**. Each slash represents one beat during which the musician should improvise. The notation below indicates four beats of improvisation.

Please note that the slashes don't necessarily indicate what rhythm you should play. For the four beats above, you could play eight eighth notes, four quarter notes, two half notes, one whole note, or any combination of those rhythms. You could also choose to rest for any or all of the beats.

Canal Street Parade Improv

The music notated below is very similar to "Canal Street Parade." The left hand "questions" are the same as the original piece, but the right hand "answers" have been replaced by slashes indicating that the pianist should improvise. Later on, we will learn fancy scales and complex tricks for improvising, but for now, focus on keeping good rhythm and improvising using these four notes:

You can use these notes in any order. You don't have to start on C. In addition to playing short notes, include long notes, repeated notes (two E's in a row, for example), and rests. But most of all, keep tapping your foot and making the music *groove*.

Remember that in a call-and-response format, the question and answer phrases should be related. Listen to each question phrase and think of a logical musical response.

If it's too tricky to improvise with the right hand while playing the left hand, have your teacher or classmate play the left-hand part for you. They can even record the left-hand part so that you can practice at home.

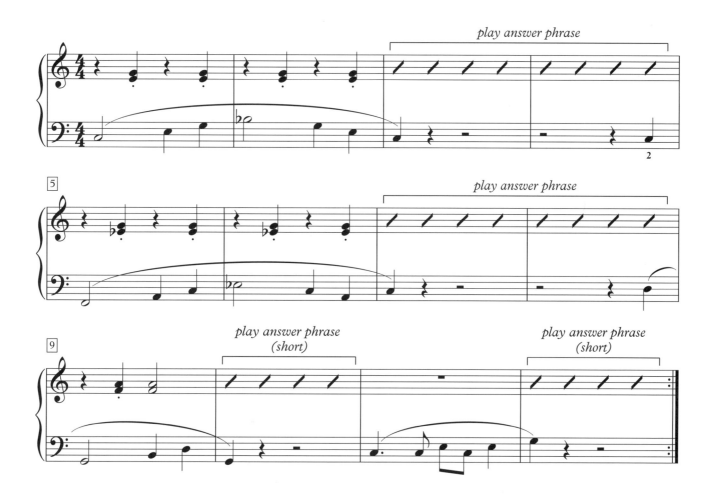

Boogie-Woogie

Boogie-woogie is a blues piano style in which the left hand plays a consistent, driving pulse. It sounds like the type of music you might hear in a cowboy movie when the hero enters the local saloon. Although boogie-woogie originated from African American pianists in the American Midwest, it was later adapted for rock 'n' roll by pianists like Jerry Lee Lewis, whose boogie-woogie hits included "Great Balls of Fire."

Typically, boogie-woogie left-hand chords include two notes each, with the top note creating a simple melody by alternating between two or three different notes. The left hand provides a rhythmic "engine" that propels the rhythm and the harmony, while the right hand is free to improvise or play a written melody.

"Drivin' a Cadillac Boogie" is named after the Cadillac, which is a classic car, just like boogie-woogie is a classic style! To give "Drivin' a Cadillac Boogie" the intensity of a fast ride on a highway, dig into the quarter-note pulse. If you can reach the first note of each measure with the suggested fingering, it will help your left hand to move more quickly and accurately.

Drivin' a Cadillac Boogie

Jeremy Siskind

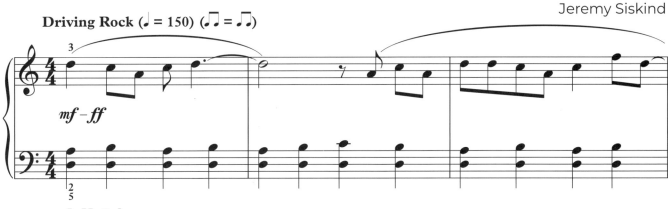

L.H. 8vb on repeat

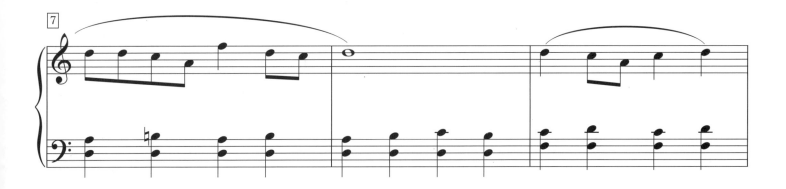

move L.H. down

Licks and Riffs

Lick is a word that musicians use to describe a short, melodic phrase. Improvising musicians often memorize standard licks in all 12 keys. A **riff** is a lick that repeats again and again. Although riffs are repetitive by nature, musicians might make small variations to riffs by changing or adding notes, especially when chords change. Musicians use both licks and riffs to play the blues. In this next piece, listen for the repeated riff in the right hand.

Echo Echo Echo Boogie

Jeremy Siskind

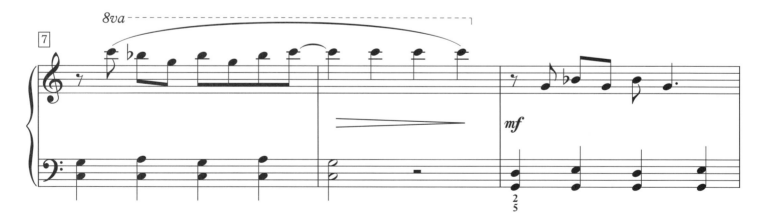

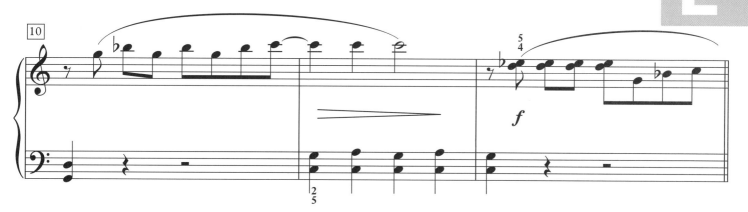

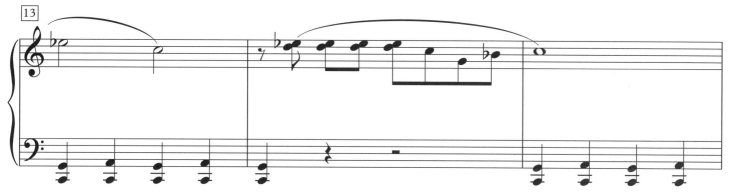

Echo Echo Echo Boogie Improv

"Echo Echo Echo Boogie" is built from two riffs. Remember, riffs are phrases that repeat with small variations. The first 12 measures are built on this riff:

From measure 13 through the end, the music is built on this riff:

Practicing inventing and playing your own riffs will help you become a better improviser. Can you write out four two-measure riffs in the measures below using the same five notes as the riffs in "Echo Echo Echo Boogie"?

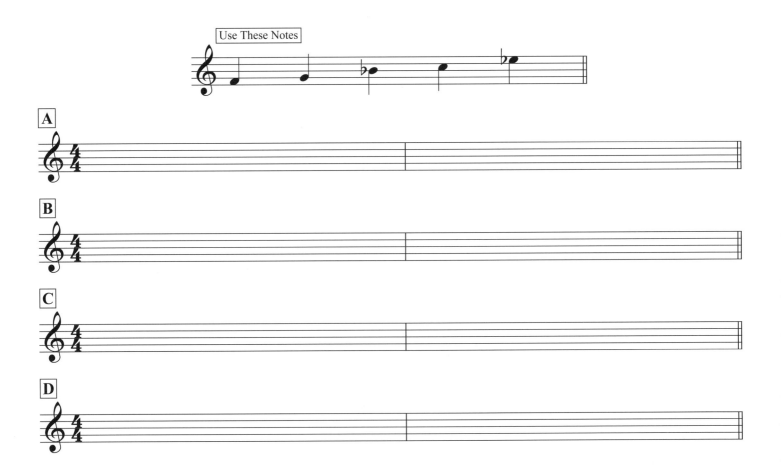

Now, practice using each riff to create a whole chorus of blues. In the piece below, the left hand is the same as "Echo Echo Echo Boogie," but the right hand has been replaced by slashes indicating improvisation.

Play your two-measure riff four times to create a melody for the first eight measures of the blues. If you'd like, you can make a small variation the second and fourth times to create some variety. For example, play the riff an octave higher or change only the last note of the riff. For the last four measures, play the original melody of "Echo Echo Echo Boogie."

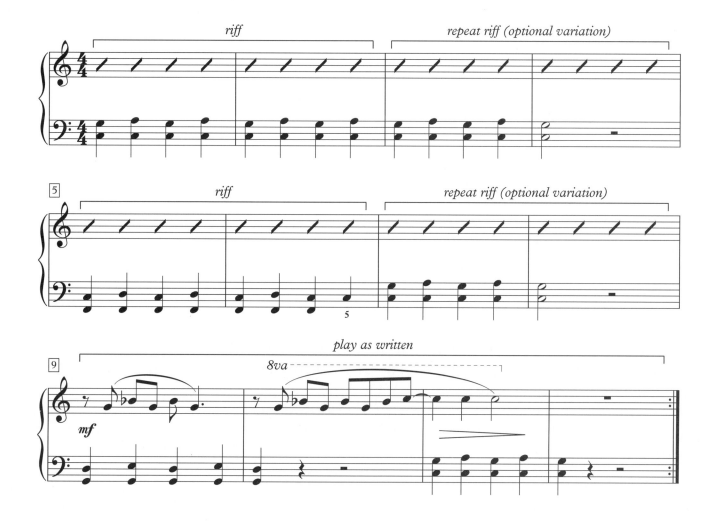

Blue Notes

Blue notes are notes from outside the traditional key center that intentionally rub up against the chord and create that gritty, bluesy feeling that is typical of blues melodies. When we name blue notes, we compare them to the notes of the major scale. The most common blue notes are the flat third, the sharp fourth, and the flat seventh.

Blue notes create tension against traditional chords. For example, play a C major chord (C-E-G) in your left hand, and then play an E-flat in your right. That's a blue note. You can hear that it "rubs" against the E natural in the chord. If you do the same thing with F-sharp and B-flat, you will hear a similar tension against different notes in the chord.

Grace Notes

Pianists often highlight the expressiveness of blue notes and other melody notes by adding **grace notes** approaching the blue note from below. These grace notes simulate a pitch bend, or **slide**, that a vocalist, guitarist, or wind player might use to add personality to a melodic phrase. Since pianos can't bend pitches, pianists use grace notes to simulate the same effect.

Play around with the timing and amount of overlap of your grace notes. Part of an artist's blues style is defined by their unique approach to grace notes – how often they use them, how quickly or slowly they play them, and how much they allow the grace notes to overlap with the main note. Although some traditional blues pianists play grace notes by sliding off a black key onto a white key using a single finger, most modern pianists opt to use different fingers for the grace note and the main note for improved control.

Fifth Avenue Blues

Jeremy Siskind

Simmering cool (♩ = 126)

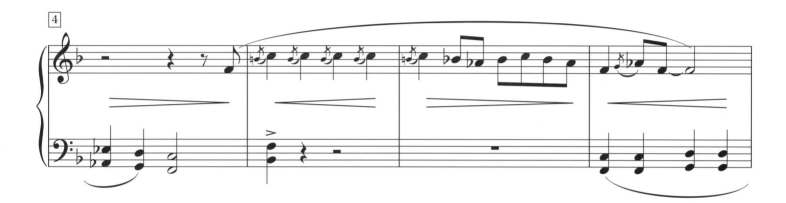

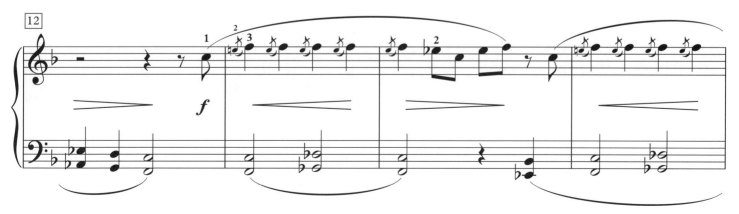

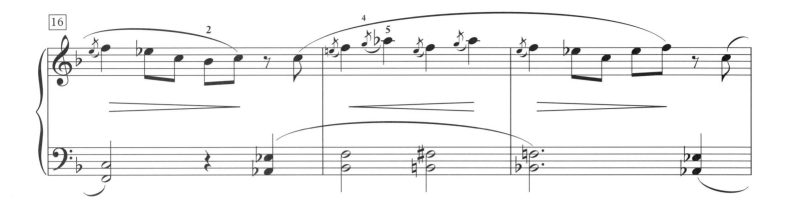

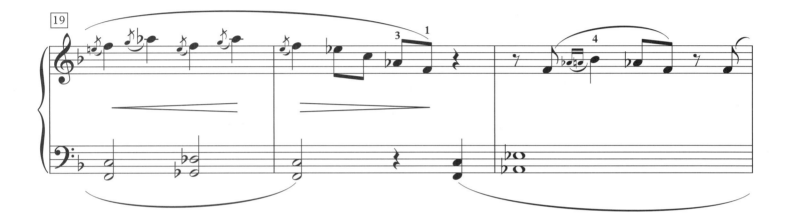

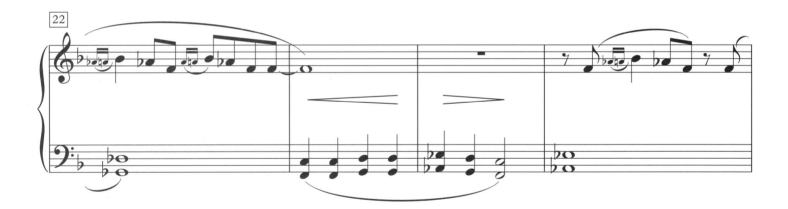

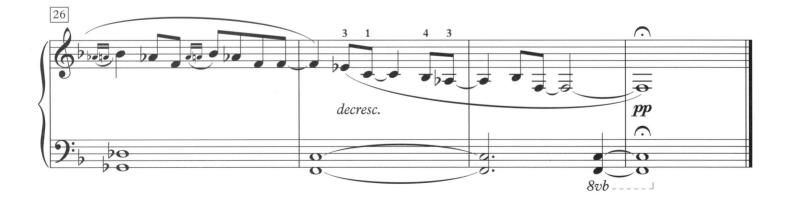

Fifth Avenue Blues Improv

Remember that we sometimes call the blues the "12-bar blues." The blues has 12 measures because it consists of three four-measure phrases (3 x 4 = 12).

Performers sometimes highlight the three phrases in the blues by giving them what we call an **AAB structure**. AAB means that the melody for the first four measures (the first "A" section) is repeated in measures five through eight (becoming the second "A" section). Then, a contrasting "B" section is added for the final four measures. If you can imagine a performer singing:

(A)   "Oh my baby left me, he left me yesterday,

(A)   Oh my baby left me, he left me yesterday,

(B)   My sweet baby got up this morning and he ran so far away."

...then you can imagine an AAB blues!

Because the AAB blues is so fundamental to the blues style, it's valuable to practice improvising an AAB blues. One key to success is that you need to *remember* what you play in the first four measures, so keep it simple and be sure to listen to yourself while you improvise.

Another key to the AAB blues is to not fill up all the space. It will work best if you make phrases that are only about two measures long and leave about two measures of rest. This **play-two, rest-two phrasing** is natural to the blues because it mirrors the call and response format discussed earlier.

Finally, make the last phrase (the "B") a clear contrast. If your two A sections have lots of short notes, use long notes in the B section. If the A sections start low and move high, start the B section high and move lower. If the A sections start right on beat one, start the B section with a rest.

Use this set of notes to improvise your AAB blues. You will recognize the left hand from "Fifth Avenue Blues."

Gospel

Gospel is a style of music associated with the African American church. It shares significant musical roots with the blues. "Gospel Sunday Blues" is a **double blues**, meaning that instead of 12 measures, the blues progression lasts 24 measures, with each chord extended for double the normal length. See if you can still hear the blues progression even with the extended rhythm.

Gospel Sunday Blues

Jeremy Siskind

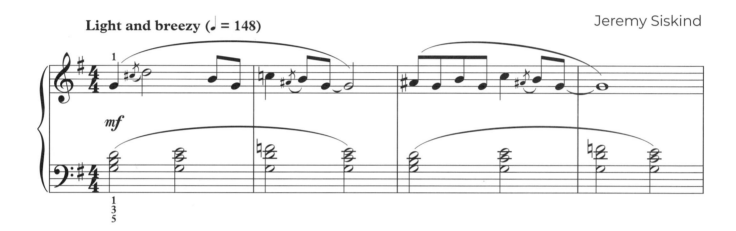

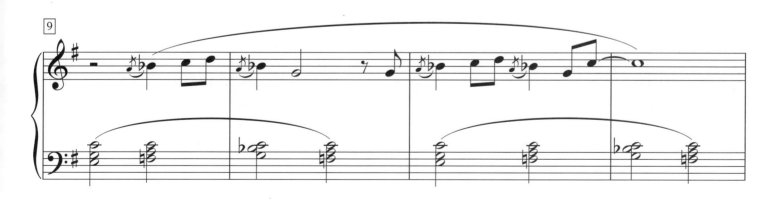

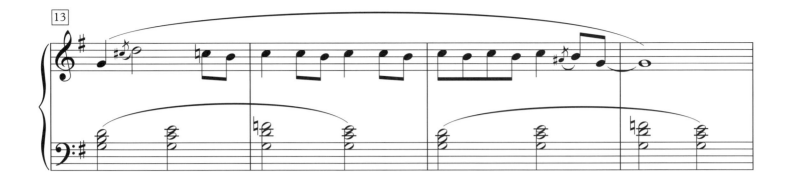

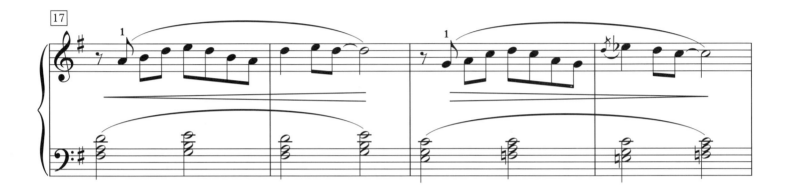

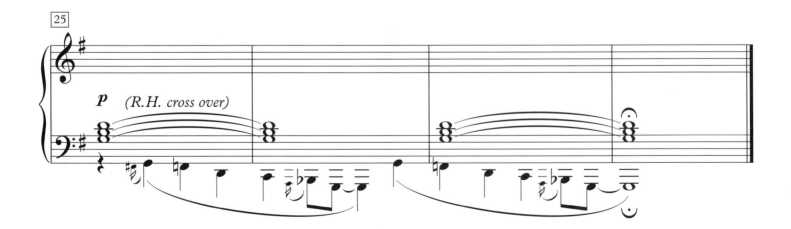

Jazz

Jazz is a style invented and refined by African American geniuses like Louis Armstrong, Duke Ellington, Charlie Parker, and Miles Davis. Although there are many different styles of jazz, most jazz is defined by improvisation, swing rhythm, and complex harmonies. Although jazz pieces use many different chord progressions, many jazz pieces are written using the blues chord progression.

There are some rhythmic elements specific to jazz that make it easily recognizable. **Swing feel** is the most unique element of jazz rhythm. Swing feel refers to the way a jazz musician plays eighth notes. To "swing" eighth notes means to lengthen the first eighth note of each pair and shorten the second note of each pair. When swinging eighth notes, the first eighth note is typically twice the length of the second.

To count swing eighth notes, instead of counting simply "one-and-two-and-three-and-four-and," you should count "one-and-a-two-and-a-three-and-a-four-and-a" with the eighth notes falling on the number (i.e. "one") and the syllable "a."

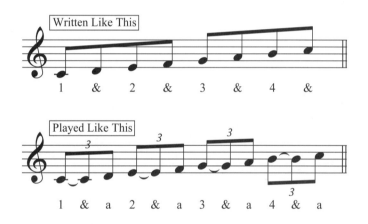

Basslines

Because jazz music is so syncopated, its basslines are rhythmically grounded. In jazz, the bass either plays constant half notes, known as a **two-feel** or **bass in two**; or it plays constant quarter notes, known as **walking bass** or **bass in four** (more on this later). Unlike other styles, basslines in jazz rarely repeat consecutive notes, instead making a smooth melody (hence the term "walking"). The piece "Half-Note Chillin'" uses a bassline in two, which feels more relaxed, or "chill," than a walking bassline.

Half-Note Chillin'

Jeremy Siskind

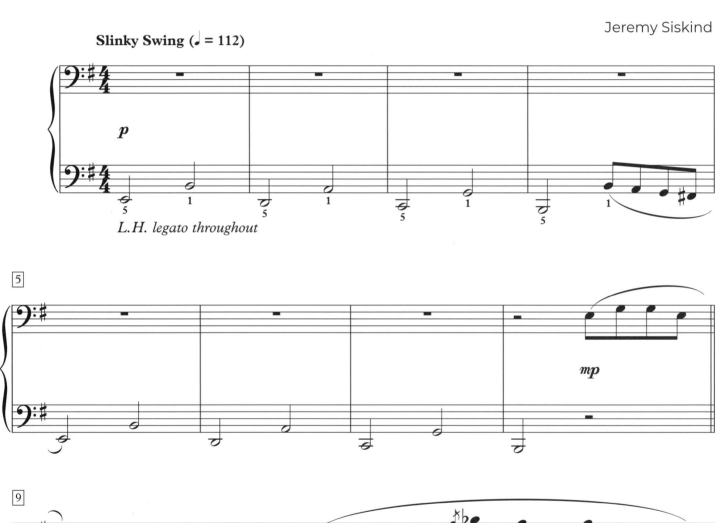

Half-Note Chillin' Improv

Just like we have a vocabulary of words when we speak, it's a good idea to start assembling a **vocabulary of rhythms** for improvisation in different styles. When learning a new style, it's smart to imitate the rhythms of pieces in that style in your improvisations.

When notating rhythms without particular notes, we write the rhythm on the middle line of the staff with "x"-es replacing circular noteheads. Here's how the first rhythm in the right hand of "Half-Note Chillin'" would be notated:

Can you write out four melodies of your own using that same rhythm? Stick with these five notes so that your melody will match the chords of "Half-Note Chillin'." Remember – you can repeat notes and move upwards or downwards at your discretion. You don't have to follow the contour of the original phrase.

Next, improvise some phrases using the same rhythm without writing them down. These phrases should sound great in "Half-Note Chillin'." Practice inserting phrases where prompted using the rhythm you practiced. If you're not sure what to play, use one of the phrases you wrote out. If it's too tricky to play the left hand while improvising with the right, have your teacher or classmate play the left-hand part for you. After a few times through, you can trade so that they're improvising the right-hand part.

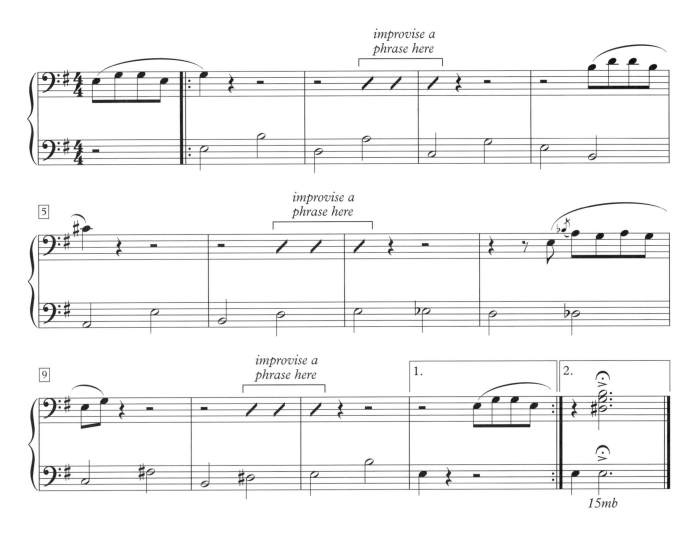

Shuffle

Shuffle is a particular type of swing feel that emphasizes the swung eighth notes with a deep groove. One difference between shuffle and swing is the way that the drums define the beat. In traditional swing, the drummer plays some of the swung eighth notes on the ride cymbal. In shuffle swing, the drummer plays all of the swung eighth notes on both the ride cymbal and the snare drum, placing a greater emphasis on the eighth-note groove. When playing a shuffle, it is essential to hear the three-part subdivision of the beat (the "one-and-a-two-and-a") in your head. In fact, "Ice Cream Drippin' Shuffle" is notated in 12/8 to help you see and feel the triple meter.

Ice Cream Drippin' Shuffle

Jeremy Siskind

Blues Scale

The **blues scale** is a collection of six notes that is often used to create melodies that fit the blues form. When naming notes in the blues scale, we compare them to the notes in a key's major scale. The blues scale consists of the root, flatted third, fourth, sharp fourth, natural fifth, and flatted seventh. Just like the major scale, it can be transposed to any key. Since the blues isn't part of the Western music tradition, this scale shouldn't be considered major or minor. It's just the blues scale.

Below, you'll see the blues scale written out in four common keys: C, F, G, and D. Can you write out the blues scale in A and E? Be sure to start with the correct major scale for each key before determining the blues scale's notes.

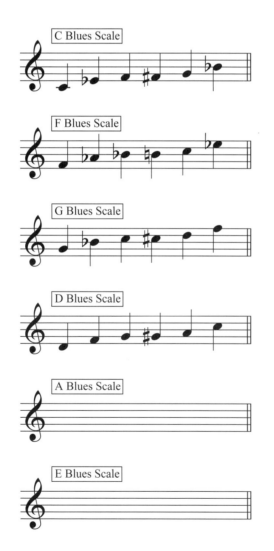

Jammin' on the Blues Scale

Jeremy Siskind

Slow Swing (♩ = 104)

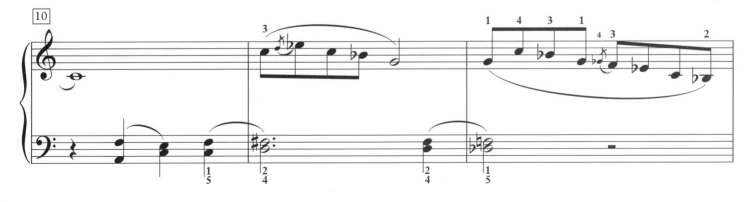

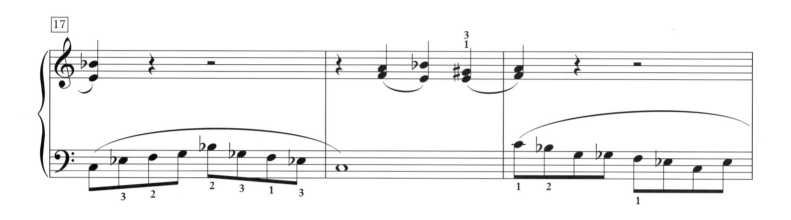

Scale Patterns

Scales provide the building blocks of improvisation. While classical musicians mostly practice playing scales up and down, jazz musicians like to practice what we call **scale patterns**, winding our way through scales in different ways. Scale patterns are often the basis of improvised melodies.

Here are a few scale patterns to practice for the C blues scale. You can practice these same patterns for the blues scale in any key:

Can you come up with your own scale patterns, mixing different numbers of notes going down and going up? You could also repeat notes or skip different notes in the scale.

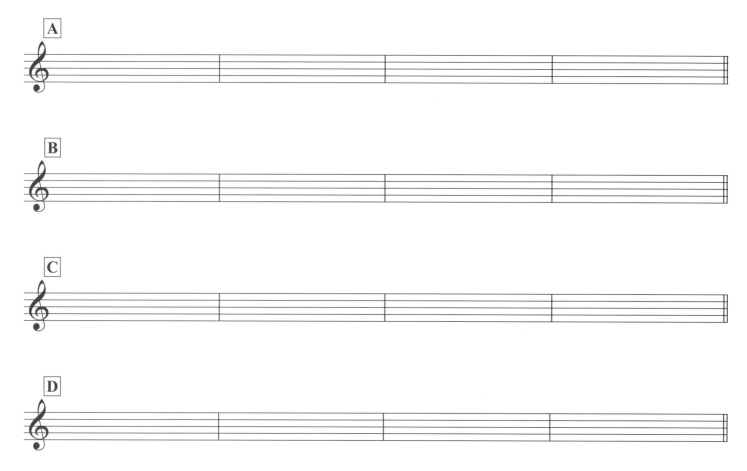

Jammin' on the Blues Scale Improv

Now that you've played some scale patterns, practice fitting them into "Jammin' on the Blues Scale." Here's how you could use pattern A for the first few measures after the introduction. Notice that the pattern was shortened in measures five and six because the whole pattern won't fit into the allotted rhythm:

Now, use Pattern C for your improvisation on "Jammin'." Because this one's so long, it has to be shortened both times to make it fit the rhythm of the piece.

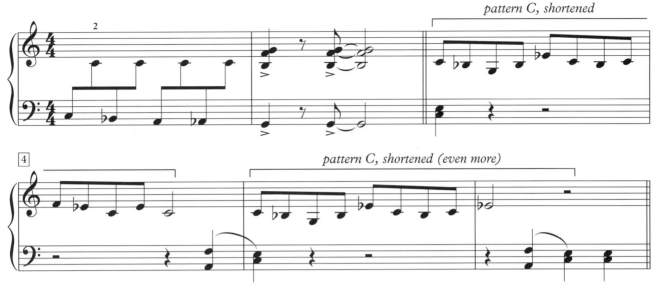

Now add your own patterns to "Jammin'." Below, you'll find prompts on where the patterns will fit best. Remember that you might have to shorten them to make them fit the rhythm. When improvising, musicians can *never* extend the number of beats in a measure to fit a melody. Melodic phrases must be lengthened or shortened to fit the length of a measure.

Sweet Scale

Another scale associated with the blues is called the **sweet scale** or the **bright blues scale**. This scale generally sounds happier than the blues scale because it includes the major third. Compared to a key's major scale, its notes are the root, second, flatted third, natural third, fifth, and sixth of the key.

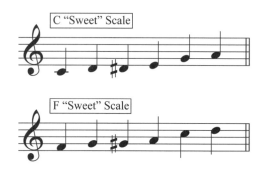

Jump Blues

The style of **jump blues**, which refers to an up-tempo blues intended for dancing, is associated with musicians like Louis Jordan and Count Basie. Basie, a pianist who started a long-running and historically important big band in Kansas City, recorded tunes like "One O'Clock Jump," "Two O'Clock Jump," and "Jump the Blues Away." The sweet scale is perfect for the jump blues because its joyfulness matches the energy of jump blues' dance rhythms.

Kansas City Jump

Jeremy Siskind

Joyful dance, swung (♩ = 164)

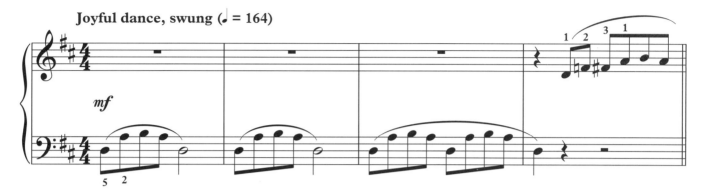

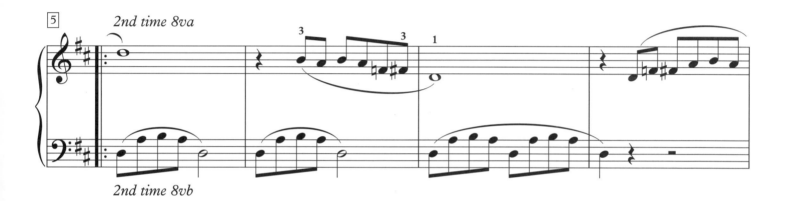

Double Notes and Turns

You can create a **double note** by adding a second note above or below the main melody note. Usually, the added note is a member of the underlying chord, such as the root or the fifth. To create tension, pianists sometimes choose a double note that's a **tritone** (a diminished fifth or augmented fourth) away from the melody note.

The feel of "Lemon Drop Shake" is meant to imitate the great James Brown, often known as the Godfather of Soul. With his top-notch funk band, Brown created hits such as "I Feel Good," "Cold Sweat," and "Hot Pants." You'll learn more about funk later in this book.

A **turn** is an ornament created by moving a step above a melody note, returning to the original melody note, and continuing downwards. Often times, turns and double notes are used in combination to create the feeling of a bent string on a guitar or a bent note from a saxophonist or vocalist. Listen to the music of piano virtuosos Oscar Peterson and Gene Harris to hear turns and double notes used expressively.

Lemon Drop Shake

Jeremy Siskind

Medium Funk (♩ = 116)

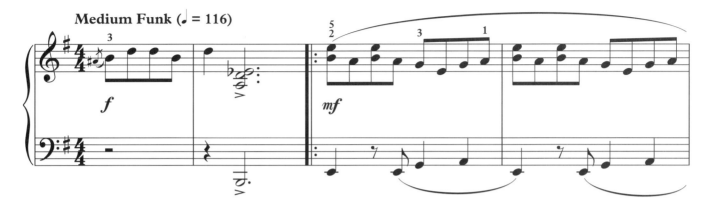

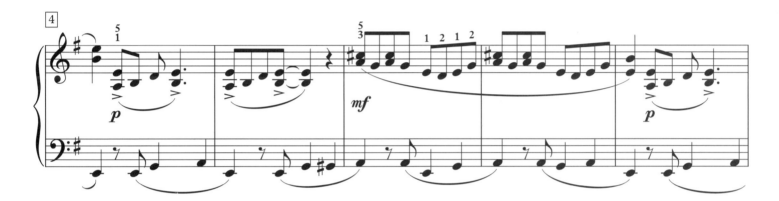

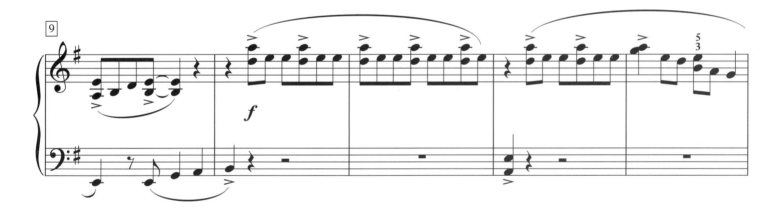

Although most of the pieces so far have used a 4/4 meter, the blues progression can be used in any time signature. "Mockingbird Waltz," which is full of turns and double notes, is written in a 3/4 meter. Like "Gospel Sunday Blues," this is a double blues, meaning that one chorus of the blues lasts 24 measures rather than the typical 12.

Mockingbird Waltz

Jeremy Siskind

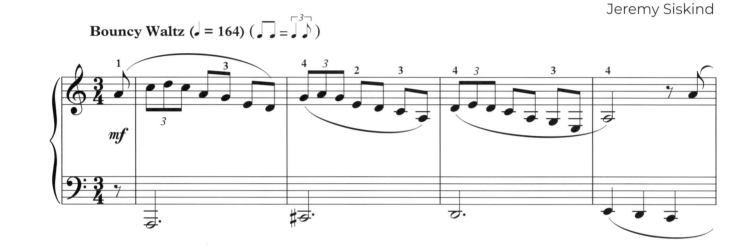

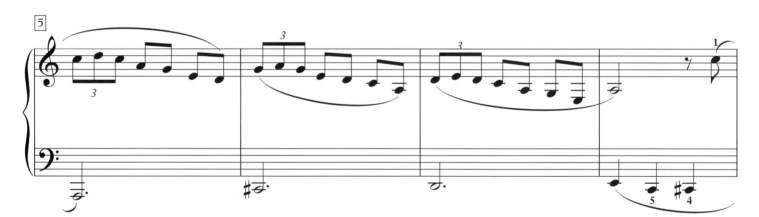

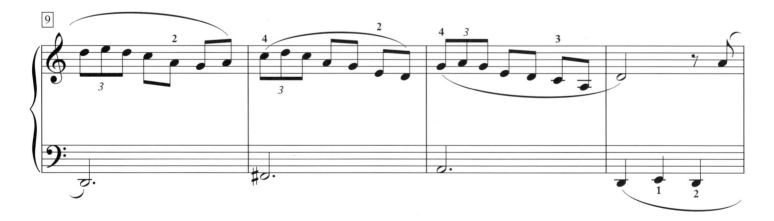

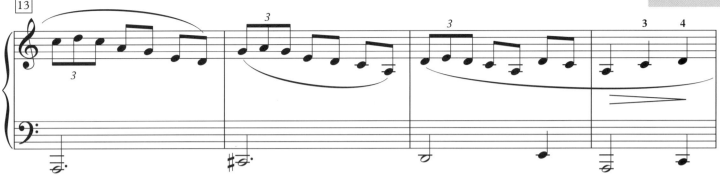

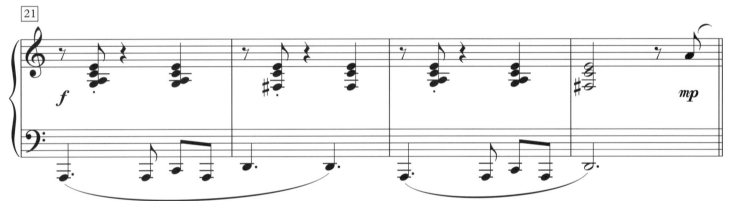

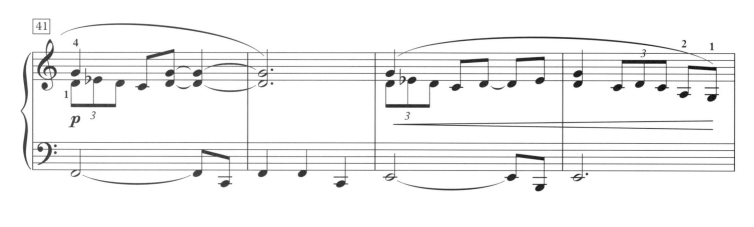

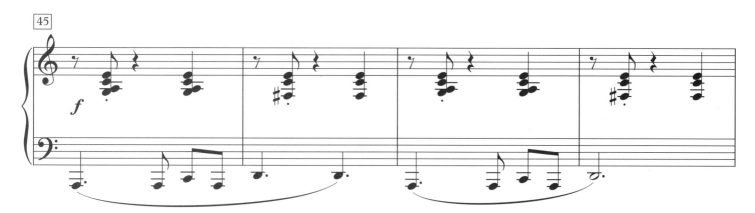

Dominant Seventh Chords

One element that's unique about the blues chord progression is that, in many styles, it's made up of exclusively dominant seventh chords. **Dominant seventh chords** are major triads with a lowered seventh added. The seventh is lowered by just a half step compared to the seventh note of the major scale. For example, a C dominant seventh chord would include the notes C, E, and G, which make up the major triad, plus B-flat, the lowered seventh.

In Western styles, such as classical music, dominant seventh chords are usually used as a tense sound that demands resolution. You might be familiar with the V7 chord, which is the most common chord that classical composers use to create musical tension. For example, in a classical piece, a C dominant seventh chord would strongly want to resolve to an F major or F minor chord. In fact, if someone played a C dominant seventh chord and then left the room, all the musicians in the room would probably be scrambling to get to the piano to play an F major or F minor chord. The tension of the chord could drive someone crazy!

Since the blues isn't a Western style, it uses dominant seventh chords in a different way. In the blues, dominant seventh chords don't necessarily have to resolve. Instead, they are presented as a stable sound.

Blues pieces can be written about things that are very emotionally profound or about everyday sadness. "New Shoes Blues" is about the very small problem that getting new shoes can hurt your feet! Listen for the dominant seventh chords which are outlined in the left hand.

New Shoes Blues

Jeremy Siskind

Laid-back groove (♩ = 98)

Chord Symbol Basics

Chord symbols are shorthand notations that tell musicians the chords for a song without having to write out the notes on a staff. Rock, blues, pop, and jazz musicians commonly use chord symbols instead of writing out notes.

To write a chord symbol for a dominant seventh chord, write the root note with a capital letter and a superscript "7." For example, to indicate an F dominant seventh chord, simply write F^7. To indicate an A-flat dominant seventh chord, write $A\flat^7$. Notice that this is an A-flat dominant chord, not an A dominant chord with a "flat 7" (which doesn't make any sense because dominant chords already have a flat seventh).

Write the chord symbols for the dominant seventh chords indicated below. The first one is done for you:

The Tango

In "Octopus Tango," look for the chord symbols above the staff. They will match the chords you play in your left hand. A **tango** is a sensual dance with origins in Latin America. It is known for its languorous, mysterious melodies. This piece is called "Octopus Tango" because you should be able to play it with only eight fingers, just like an octopus has eight arms. You don't need to use your right hand pinky or your left-hand fourth finger.

Octopus Tango

Jeremy Siskind

Slinky and mysterious (♩ = 116)

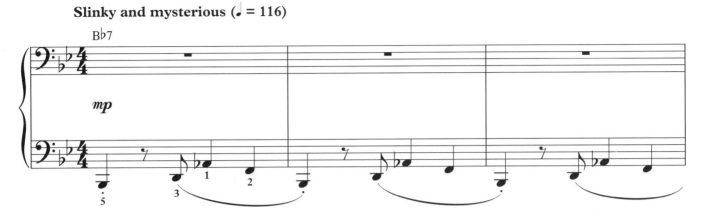

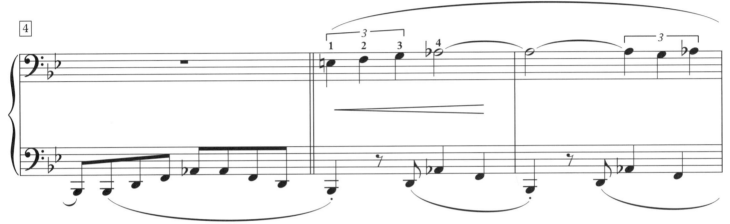

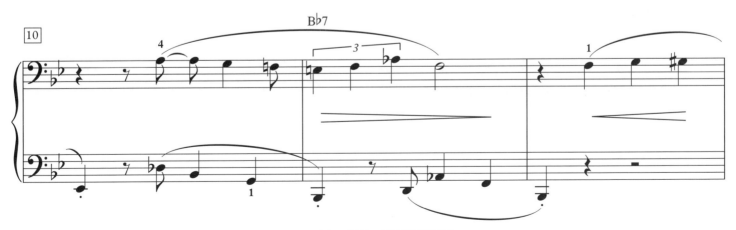

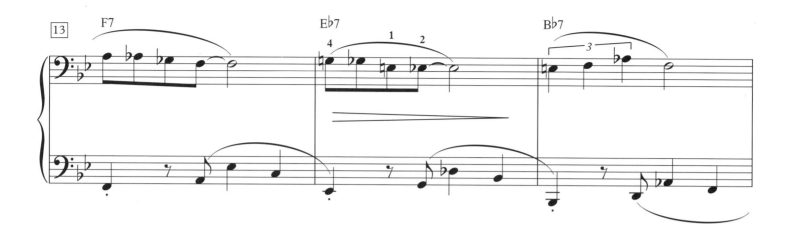

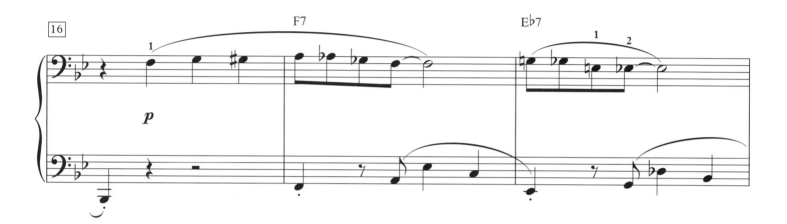

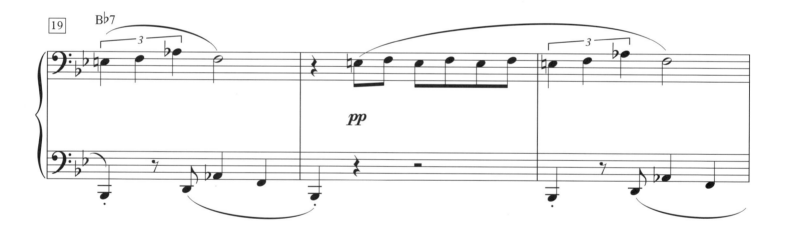

Comping

Improvising isn't always about creating a new melody. Improvising an accompaniment is called **comping**. The word "comping" is an abbreviation for "accompanying." The slashes used for melodic improvisation are the same slashes to indicate comping; however, notation for comping will include a chord symbol:

To "comp" appropriately, you need to learn common rhythms for different styles and combine the rhythms with the chords indicated by the chord symbol. Below are three common comping rhythms for jazz styles. For the **Freddie Green** comping rhythm, play the chord lightly on every beat. Freddie Green was a guitarist with the Count Basie orchestra known for strumming quarter notes. For the **Charleston** rhythm, named after a 1920s dance craze, comp short chords on beat one and the "and of two." For the **Reverse Charleston**, play short chords on the "and of one" and beat three.

On the left-hand side of the example below, you will see comping indicated for a dominant chord. On the right-hand side, you'll see how you would play that chord in the indicated style. Although you could play the notes in any register, you want to keep them roughly in the octave below middle C so that they neither get so low that they become muddy, nor so high that they conflict with the melody.

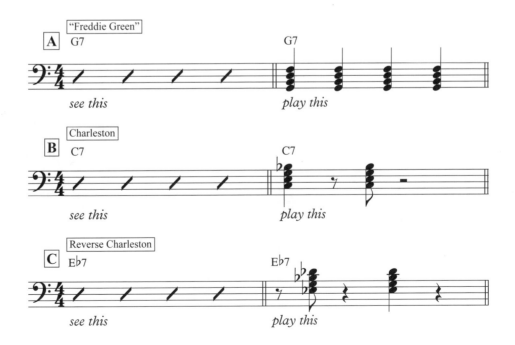

Octopus Tango Improv

Now, pretend that you wanted to play "Octopus Tango" in a jazz style rather than as a tango. For the piece below, practice comping in the three patterns mentioned above using the chords and melody of "Octopus Tango." You can even mix the comping rhythms – do a couple measures of Freddie Green style comping, then one measure of Charleston, and one measure of Reverse Charleston, etc. Note that the melody has been written an octave higher than it was played previously to give your left hand more room.

If the coordination is too tricky, have your teacher or classmate play the melody while you practice comping.

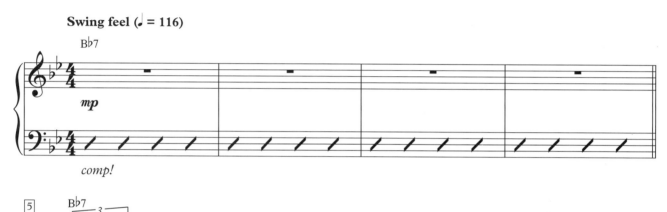

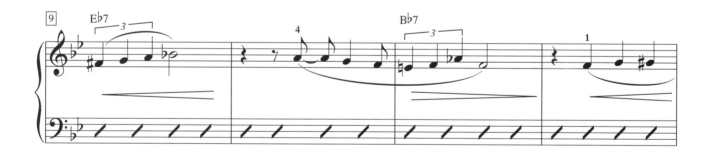

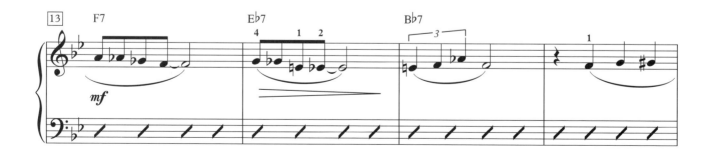

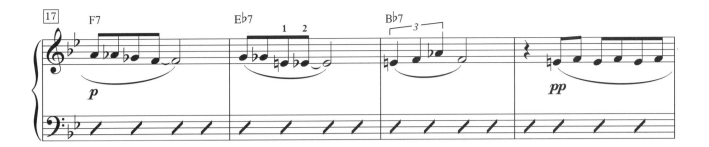

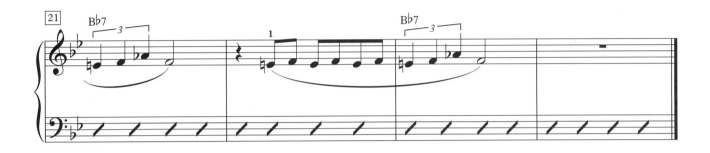

Inversions

Math lovers everywhere know that March fourteenth is "Pi Day." It's the celebration of the mathematical constant pi, also known as **π**, which appears often in mathematical equations. The first three digits of pi are 3.14, or 3-14, so it's only natural that Pi Day is celebrated on March 14th. "Pi Day Blues" uses those three digits to create a blues melody. Set in the key of D, the melodic motif is created from the third, first, and fourth notes of the D major scale, or 3-1-4. Those of you who are really into math will find a secret pi-related code in measures nine through twelve.

In "Pi Day Blues," you'll see some chord symbol notation you haven't seen before. First, you will see just letter names, with no "7" added. These letter names mean that you're playing that key's major triad. For example, when you see the chord symbol "D," you will be playing a D major triad. The other new notation is a diagonal line. In chord symbols, diagonal lines are used to notate **inversions**, chords with a note other than the root as the lowest note. When you see a chord such as "D/A," it should be read as "D over A," or a D major triad with A as the lowest note.

Walking Bass

Walking bass, or "bass in four," is a melodic bassline style in which the bass plays four quarter notes per measure (see also page 28). Walking bass is a common bassline for jazz in a swing feel. Walking basslines should be played legato, with slight accents on beats two and four. These accents replace the hi-hat cymbals, which the drummer typically plays using his foot on beats two and four.

The walking bass starts on the second chorus of "Pi Day Blues." Notice that the notes in the walking bass don't always cleanly line up with the notes indicated in the chord symbols. Using notes outside of the chord to create a flowing melody is a normal part of the walking bass style.

Pi Day Blues

Jeremy Siskind

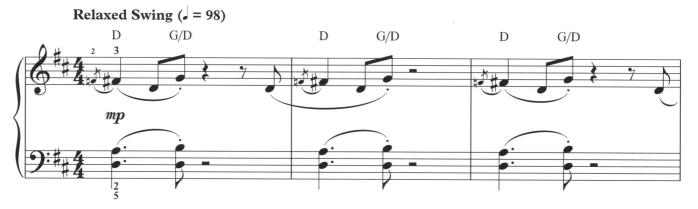

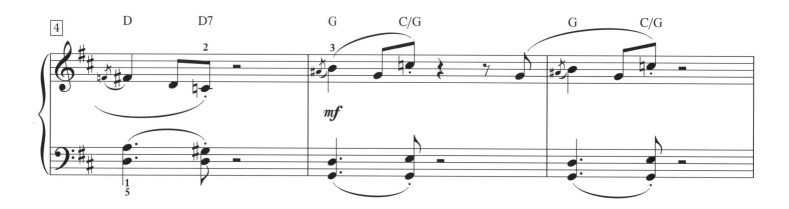

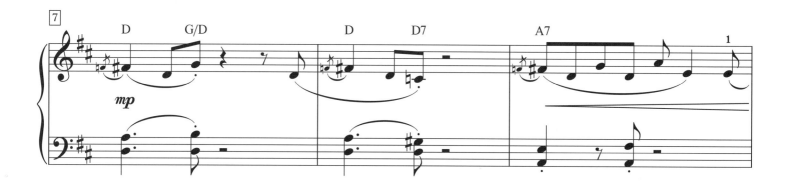

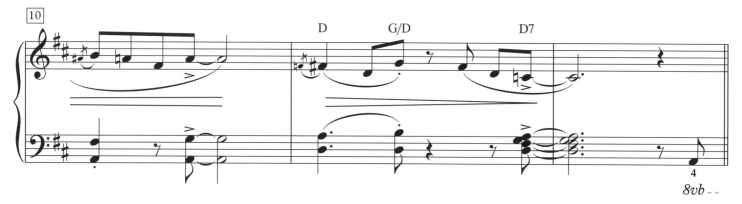

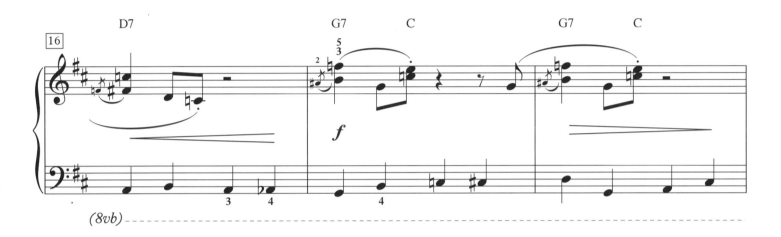

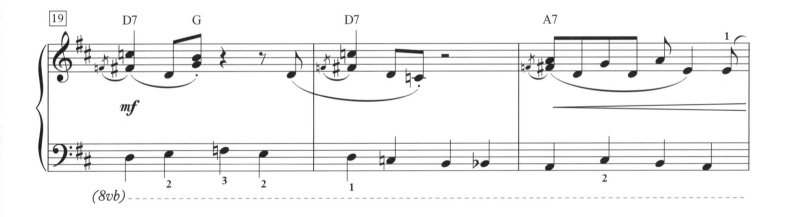

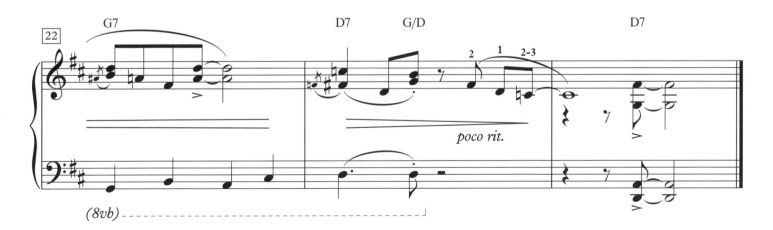

When playing "Quarter-Note Walkin'," keep the bassline legato and put a slight accent on the quarter notes on beats two and four. In this piece, we will add one new chord symbol to our repertoire. The "Cm7" means "C minor seventh." A minor seventh chord is a chord with a minor triad, and the same lowered seventh that we add to a dominant seventh chord. The notes for a C minor seventh chord are C, E-flat, G, and B-flat. Using minor seventh chords in the blues is more common in the jazz version of the blues than in rock, funk, or soul.

Quarter-Note Walkin'

Jeremy Siskind

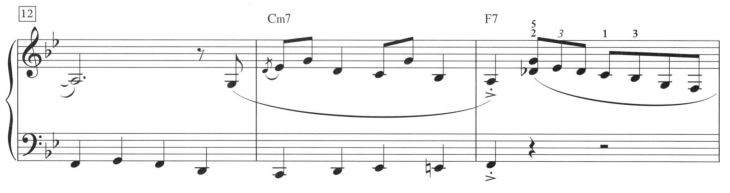

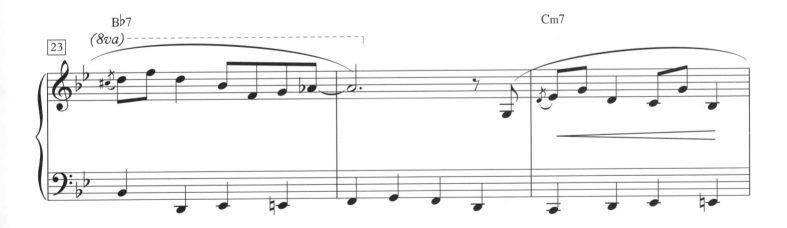

Quarter-Note Walkin' Improv

Besides the two blues scales that we learned earlier, you can choose to use the notes of the chords for your improvisation. You might have noticed the melody of "Quarter-Note Walkin'" uses the notes of the chords in the melody as they change. Look at the diagram below:

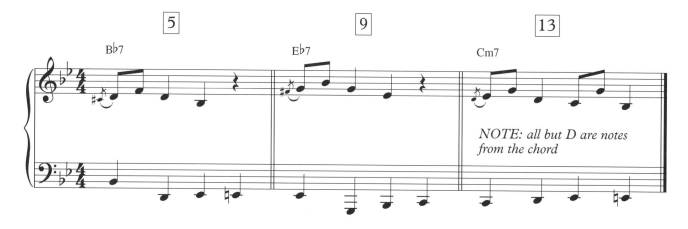

When we use the notes of a chord to make a single-note melody, we call it **arpeggiating** the chord. You might have practiced arpeggios for your lessons, which, if you think about it, create a single-note melody going up and down the piano using notes of a chord.

Arpeggiating the chords is a little bit trickier than using the blues scale because you have to know when to change chords. Before you improvise over the chord progression of "Quarter-Note Walkin'," improvise over each chord individually. When you see a B-flat dominant seventh chord, you can use the notes B-flat, D, F, and A-flat in any rhythm, any octave, with repetitions, skips, and grace note slides. Don't forget to include rests. Here's a sample improvisation over *just* the B-flat dominant seventh chord.

Practice improvising using the notes of the first two chords from "Quarter-Note Walkin'," given below. See if you can improvise on each chord for thirty seconds without getting bored.

Now it's time to improvise on the chord progression of "Quarter-Note Walkin'." Have your teacher or classmate play the accompaniment and use the notes of the chords to improvise where indicated. When you get to the C minor seventh and F dominant seventh chords, improvise using the blues scale. For now, those chords probably go by too quickly to use our new technique. Be sure to count the measures as they go by so that you switch chords at the right time.

Funk

Funk is a musical style with roots in the blues and the gospel church that is typified by blues-based harmonies, complex cross-rhythms, and intricate basslines. Great funk artists and bands include Parliament, James Brown, Maceo Parker, Sly and the Family Stone, and Earth, Wind & Fire.

One typical chord in funk music is the **sharp nine chord**. The sharp nine chord looks like it has both major and minor thirds. In fact, the "minor third" is the raised ninth scale degree. That's right, even though pianists usually think of scales as having only eight notes, you could continue past that eighth note to the ninth note, which is the same as the second scale degree. Musicians prefer to call it the ninth because the other notes of the chord are all odd (the root, third, fifth, seventh, etc.). Raising that note gives you the sharp nine, which is enharmonically equivalent to the minor third.

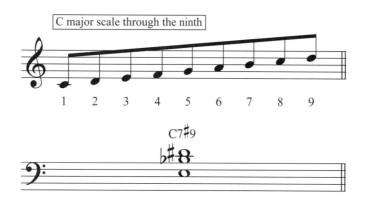

"Rattle and Roll" is a double blues written in the funk style. Even though there are some chords that sound dissonant when held or played slowly, if played at an appropriate tempo, they'll sound colorful and stylistically appropriate. Imagine a horn section playing the tight voicings that make up the melody.

Rattle and Roll

Jeremy Siskind

Medium Funk groove (♩ = 127)

Another device that pianists use in gospel, funk, and soul is **second inversion triads**, triads with the fifth of the chord on bottom. In "Summer Evening Blues," watch for the second inversion triads that harmonize the melody. Even though it's meant to evoke a peaceful summer night, the piece is notated with sixteenth notes, which is typical of the funk and soul genres.

Summer Evening Blues

Jeremy Siskind

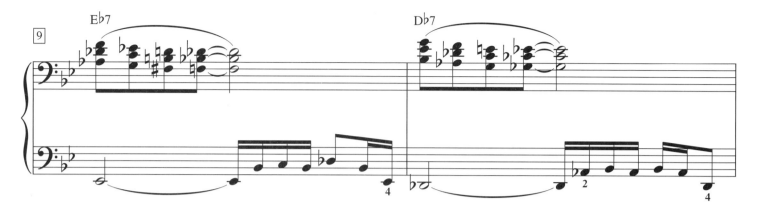

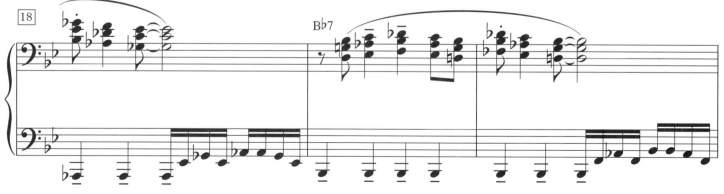

Eighth-Note Boogie-Woogie

Earlier, you played basic boogie-woogie pieces to get the hang of a left-hand accompaniment with a consistent "engine." You are now ready to tackle more complex boogie-woogie based on eighth-note lines in the left hand, which is more typical of how the great boogie-woogie pianists performed. There are so many fun patterns created by legends like Clarence "Pine Top" Smith, Meade "Lux" Lewis, Albert Ammons, and Pete Johnson. "Twisty-Turny Boogie" uses two popular boogie-woogie patterns, one that simply doubles the quarter-note pattern used in "Drivin' a Cadillac Boogie," and one that's much more athletic for the left hand. Practice hands separately before putting them together because the melodies for both hands are "twisty" and "turny."

Twisty-Turny Boogie

Jeremy Siskind

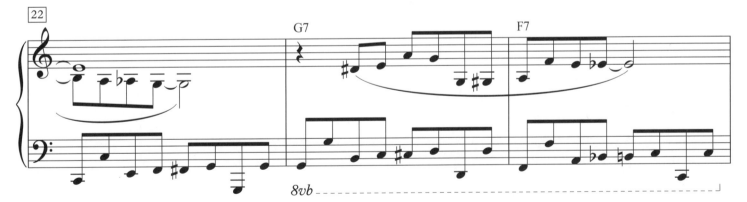

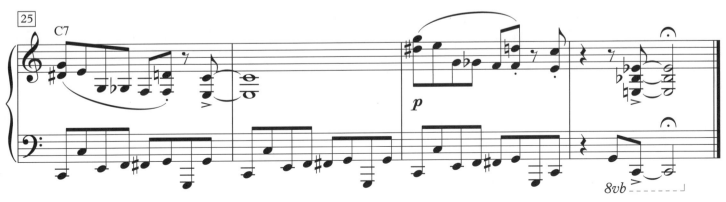

Ascending Leaps

Because blues is such an inherently expressive artform, it's important for improvisers to consider how to make blues improvisations expressive. One way to make a melody expressive is by using **ascending leaps**. Oddly, the piano is one of the few instruments for which going higher is not more difficult. If you think of a vocalist, trumpeter, or violinist, playing in the upper register is actually more physically taxing than playing in the middle range. Therefore, listeners hear a sudden shift to the upper register as being highly emotionally charged. If you think about great melodies, whether it's Chopin's famous Nocturne in E-flat Major or "Somewhere Over the Rainbow," many of them feature large leaps.

Leaping large intervals can be a little uncomfortable for improvisers who are used to practicing scales, which, by definition, move by step. The easiest leap to start with is an octave leap, because you can be confident that if the pitch that starts the leap sounds okay, the pitch an octave up will sound good as well. After all, they're the same pitch!

You can also map out some other leaps that will sound good. Here are a few leaps that fit with "Twisty-Turny Boogie," drawn from the C blues scale. These expressive leaps are larger than a fifth.

When playing a leap in the blues, it's extra expressive to emphasize the "struggle" in the leap. Although it's no harder to play higher than lower on the piano, pretend that you're playing a wind instrument that makes playing that high note really difficult. To emphasize the exertion of the higher note, use grace notes to slide into the note and experiment with timing the note just a little bit late in order to highlight the effort.

Twisty-Turny Boogie Improv

Using the C blues scale, improvise using these expressive leaps over the accompaniment from "Twisty-Turvy Boogie," maintaining play-two, rest-two phrasing. Have your teacher or classmate play the accompaniment at first, then see if you can put hands together.

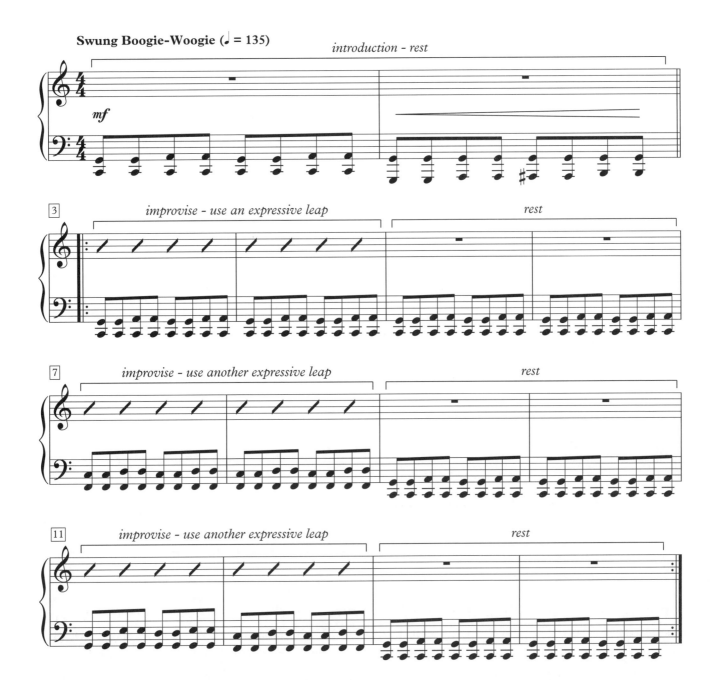

One way to expand upon the play-two, rest-two phrasing is to play in the second half of each phrase instead of the first half. Improvise as directed in the example below:

"Ubuntu" is a Bantu word that is literally translated as "I am because we are." Although Ubuntu philosophy is complex, it's rooted in the belief that there's a universal bond that connects all humanity. The "Ubuntu Boogie" uses a left-hand pattern that might look simple at first but, upon closer inspection, is rhythmically tricky. Most musicians are accustomed to playing the bass notes on the beat and the chords on the offbeats, but in this pattern, the bass notes are on the offbeats and the chords are played on the beat. Until you get used to it, you might feel like your hands are playing in two different meters altogether!

"Ubuntu Boogie" needs to be played with a **shuffle swing**, meaning a swing feel that's precisely locked into the triplet feel. Subdivide the triplets in the measure and follow the articulation carefully. Very sharp, short staccatos are appropriate for the shuffle swing style.

Ubuntu Boogie

Jeremy Siskind

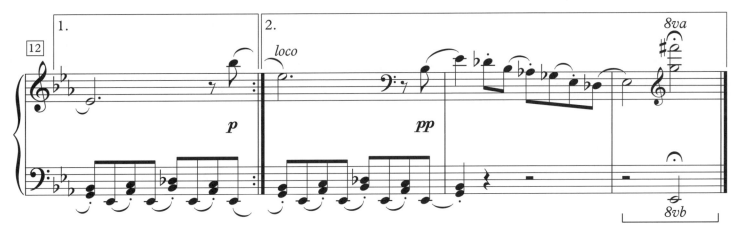

Bebop

Bebop is a complex musical language developed in the 1940s and '50s by African American geniuses like Charlie Parker, Dizzy Gillespie, Bud Powell, and Thelonious Monk. Bebop is known for its harmonic sophistication, unpredictable rhythms, and jagged melodic shapes.

Bebop musicians frequently reinvented popular chord progressions, including the blues, with heightened sophistication. Many of the most famous pieces written by bebop musicians use the blues form, including "Billie's Bounce," "Blues for Alice," "Blue Monk," and "Relaxin' at Camarillo."

In fact, Charlie Parker, whose nickname was "Bird," wrote so many blueses that jazz musicians call a special version of the blues that uses bebop chords a **Bird Blues**. As you play through "Vulture's Blues," notice all of the different sounds that are added to the blues progression, as well as the jagged melodic shapes characteristic of bebop.

Major Seventh Chord

In "Vulture's Blues," you'll encounter a new chord symbol, the **major seventh chord**, written as "maj7." A major seventh chord takes the first, third, fifth, and seventh notes from the major scale of the root. For example, an A♭maj7 consists of A♭, C, E♭, and G. You'll also encounter a new kind of bassline that is less predictable than a bassline in two or four. Because it "breaks up" the time, this kind of unpredictable bassline is called a **broken-feel bassline**.

Vulture's Blues

Jeremy Siskind

Bouncy Swing (♩ = 138)

L.H. legato, accent off-beats

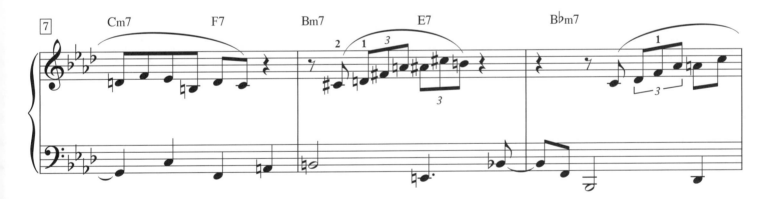

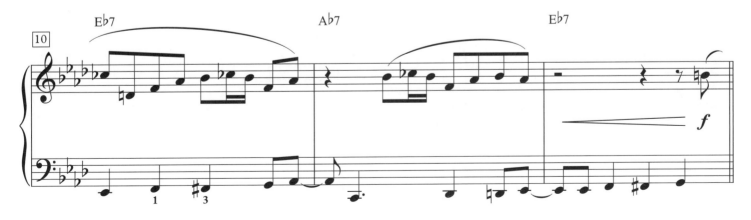

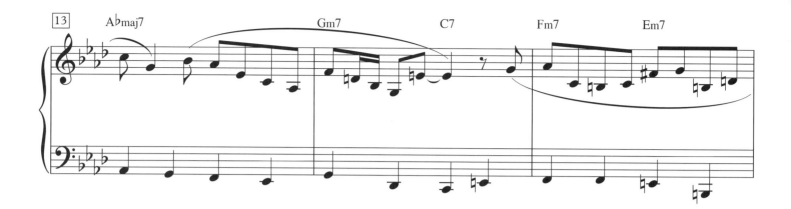

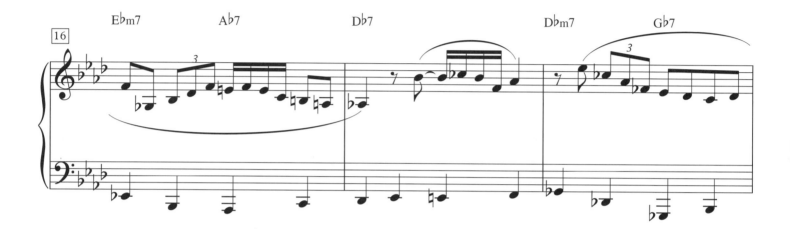

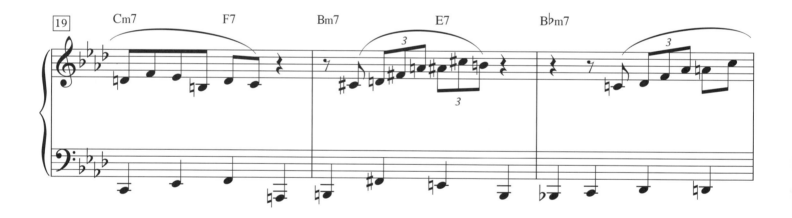

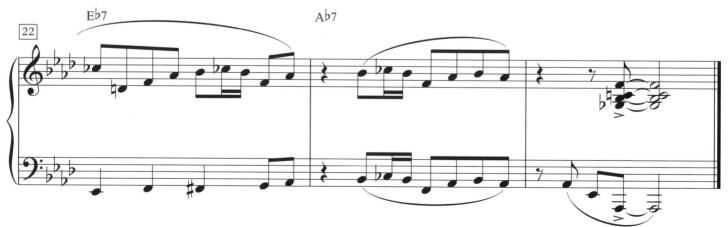

Vulture's Blues Improv

So where would you even start if you wanted to improvise on a tune with as many chords as "Vulture's Blues"? One place to start is with arpeggios. Because the chords move so quickly, find the arpeggios in inversions where you can move smoothly from one chord to the next.

Once you can play these chords in rhythm, use the hand positions as a basis for your improvised melody. For example, for the first four measures, you could play either of the following options, which only use the notes from the chords above. Notice that you don't have to use all of the notes in every chord.

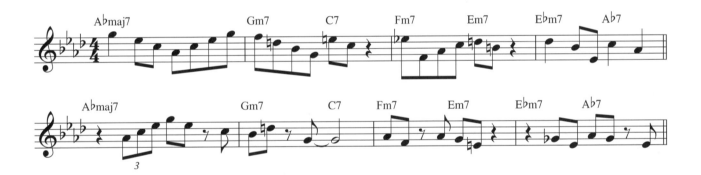

If you get bored with the notes from these hand positions, add a **half-step lead-in** from below any of the notes of the chord. These lead-ins add color and are typical of the bebop style.

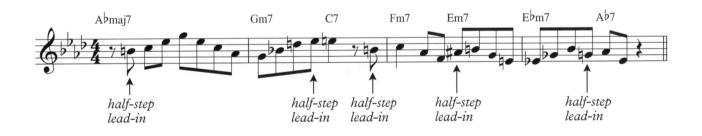

Now that you've got the hang of the first four measures, write out the hand positions for measures 5 through 12 of the chord progression for "Vulture's Blues." Feel free to leap up by an octave if you start getting too low.

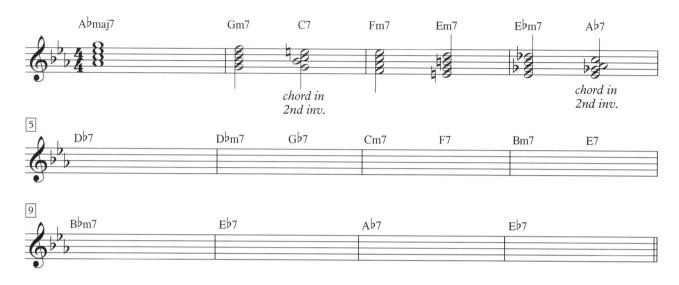

Once you've got your hand positions solidly down, improvise with the right hand over the chord progression of "Vulture's Blues" while your teacher or classmate plays the left-hand part.

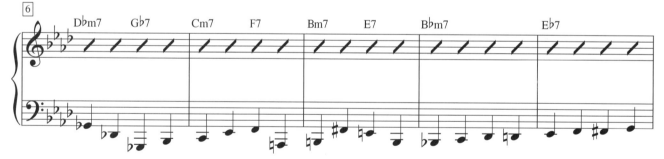

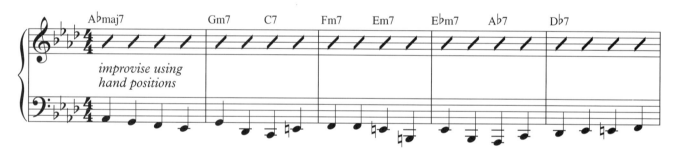

Thelonious Monk

Of all the bebop musicians, **Thelonious Monk** is probably the most unique. In fact, one of his best albums is called *The Unique*. Monk had an amazing way of making dissonant chords actually sound pleasant, or if not pleasant, at least, hip. His melodies are jagged, unpredictable, and usually saturated with a single motif.

"Well, You Oughta" is loosely based on Monk's piece called "Well, You Needn't." It's a **blues with a bridge**, a form in which the 12-bar blues is used as the A section in an AABA form. In "Well, You Oughta," you'll play the blues twice, then an alternate section, called a **bridge**, then the blues once more. Famous examples of blues-with-a-bridge pieces are "Locomotion" by John Coltrane and "Unit Seven" by Sam Jones, made famous by Julian "Cannonball" Adderley.

Whole Tone Scale

In the bridge of "Well, You Oughta," you'll notice another one of Monk's trademarks, the **whole tone scale**. The whole tone scale is a scale made up of only whole steps and is often used in television and film to accompany a dream sequence.

The quirkiness of the scale fits Monk's style perfectly!

Well, You Oughta

Jeremy Siskind

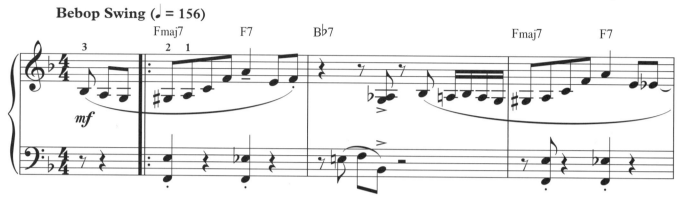

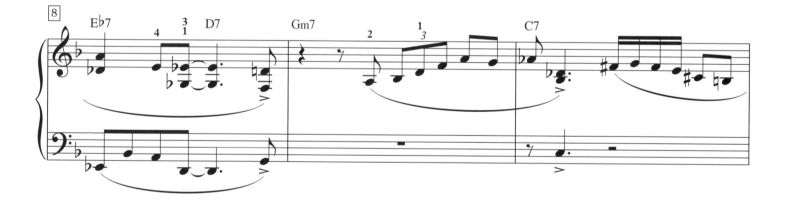

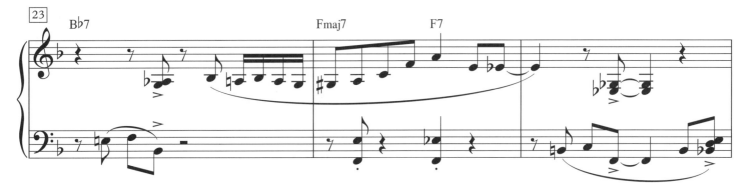

(use both hands)
8va- - - -

Modal Blues

If bebop was the most important jazz innovation of the '40s and '50s, **modal jazz** was the new innovation of the '60s. A **mode** is a collection of notes created by starting a scale from a note other than the root. For example, if you play the C major scale from D to D, you get the D Dorian mode; from E to E, you get E Phrygian; from F to F, you get F Lydian; and so on. Each of these modes has a different musical character.

Many jazz musicians mix these modes with the blues. Most famously, Wayne Shorter wrote tunes like "Footprints" and "Witch Hunt" that don't take place in major or minor, but instead, feature a Dorian mode as the home sound. More modern musicians like Chick Corea ("Matrix") and Kenny Garrett ("Wooden Steps") have written modal blues pieces.

The next piece, "Xerxes' Phrygian Lament," is based on the Phrygian mode, which is associated with Spanish music. The Phrygian mode's distinctive sound comes from the half step between the first and second scale degree. The left-hand part features **quartal voicings**, voicings based around the interval of a fourth, which are common in modal jazz. These voicings were standardized by McCoy Tyner, the pianist in John Coltrane's famed quartet.

"Xerxes' Phrygian Lament" was named after Xerxes I, a Persian King who ruled over the territory of Hellespontine Phrygia, namesake of the Phrygian mode! Ancient Phrygia is now located in the Asian portion of modern-day Turkey.

Xerxes' Phrygian Lament

Jeremy Siskind

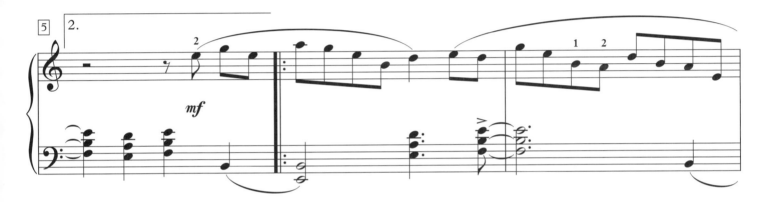

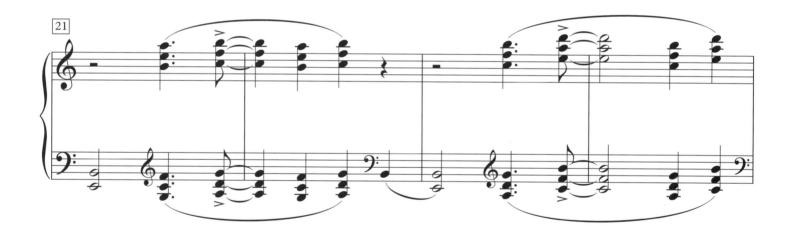

Xerxes' Phrygian Lament Improv

Use the Phrygian modes for E and A when improvising over "Xerxes' Phrygian Lament." Here are the notes of those two modes, which are based on the C major and F major scales:

When improvising with modes, it's important to include a variety of intervals and melodic shapes. To this end, practice the modes in different scale patterns, especially patterns with skips between notes. Here are a few examples for the E Phrygian mode:

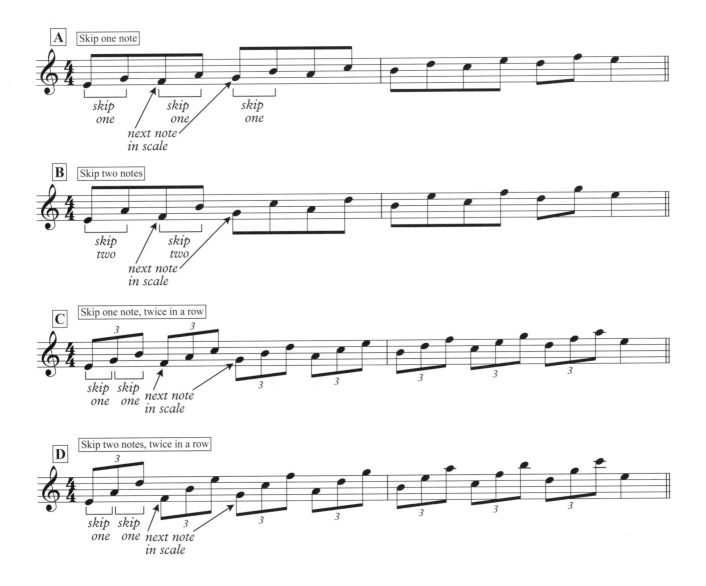

To achieve true mastery, practice improvising in constant eighth notes in each mode for a minute around ♩ = 75 beats per minute. Play only notes in the mode and resist defaulting to patterns. Make it as varied as possible. Varied hand positions will result in more interesting melodies. Be sure to cross over and under as you improvise, just as you would when playing scales.

Improvise on "Xerxes' Phrygian Lament" while your teacher or classmate plays the accompaniment. Even though you've practiced playing constant eighth notes with these modes, strive to create interesting rhythms to complement the melodic shapes you've been practicing. Because measure 9 and 10 are very tricky for improvising, play the original melody whenever you arrive at that part of the piece.

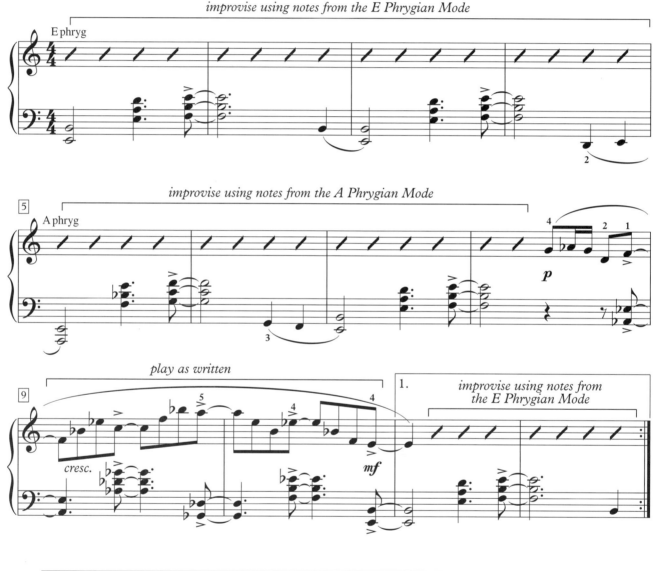

Hemiolas and Tremolos

These last two pieces are funky in style and written more as "improvisations" than songs. In other words, you probably couldn't sing either of these pieces, but they're sure fun to listen to and play!

Jimmy Yancey's legendary boogie-woogie piece, "Yancey Special," has a different kind of boogie-woogie left hand that's not based on the consistent engine of repeated quarter notes or eighth notes. Instead, Yancey plays a loping bass figure and improvises over the top. "Yancey's Revenge" takes that figure and layers different melodic lines over the bass. In particular, this piece utilizes **hemiolas**, rhythmic groupings that don't fit cleanly into the overall meter, but instead create rhythmic tension. "Yancey's Revenge" also uses **tremolos**, alternations between two notes in a single hand to create a "shaking" effect.

"Yancey's Revenge" is supposed to feel ragged and improvised, so don't stress too much about the difference between the rhythmic units here. Although the swing feel is notated in an older style that emphasizes the very relaxed swing feel of the left-hand pattern, the right-hand triplets should line up to the left-hand rhythm, even though, technically, they don't align.

Yancey's Revenge

Jeremy Siskind

Relaxed Boogie-Woogie (♩ = 88)

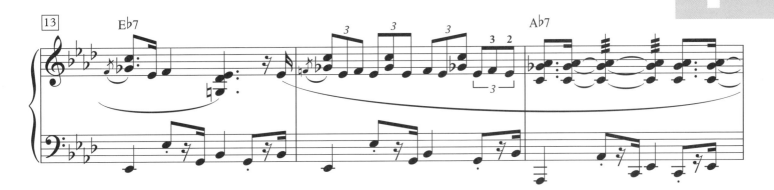

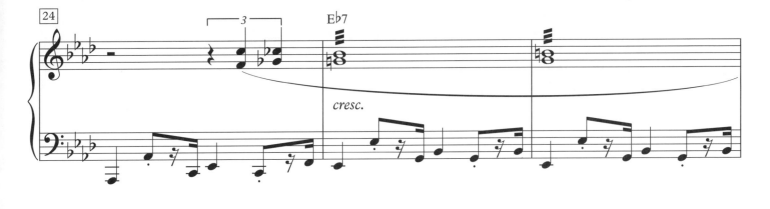

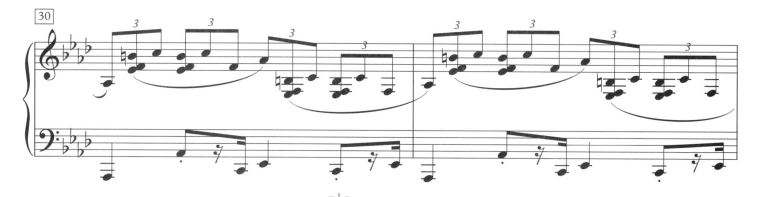

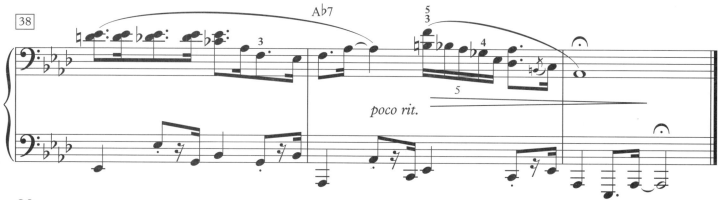

New Orleans Piano Tradition

Although we already visited New Orleans before for "Canal Street Parade," it's worth one more trip to the French Quarter to play a piece inspired by New Orleans pianists Dr. John, Allen Touissant, Fats Domino, Jon Batiste, and Professor Longhair. The New Orleans piano tradition combines elements of boogie-woogie, jazz, rock 'n' roll, funk, and borrows rhythmic and cultural elements from the voodoo island traditions.

Zydeco is a music native to Louisiana that also combines disparate elements into a unique musical output. Zydeco is often performed by musicians playing accordions, violins, and a "vest frottoir," a special washboard worn over the shirt. Although "Zydeco Strut" isn't quite traditional zydeco, it draws upon a lot of the same roots.

To get the rhythmic feel right for this piece, it is essential to stomp your foot on all four quarter notes of the measure. Here, the slurs mark phrasing only – play the eighth note octaves in the left hand non-legato – not short but not connected. Lastly, New Orleans piano tends to emphasize beat one, the "and of two," and beat four, so don't be afraid to lean into those beats. Watch for a **stop time** section in the second chorus in which the accompaniment stops to allow for virtuosic right-hand fills.

Zydeco Strut

Jeremy Siskind

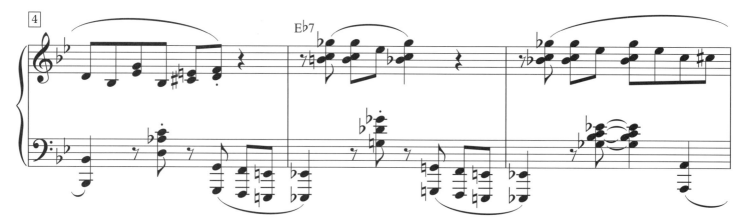

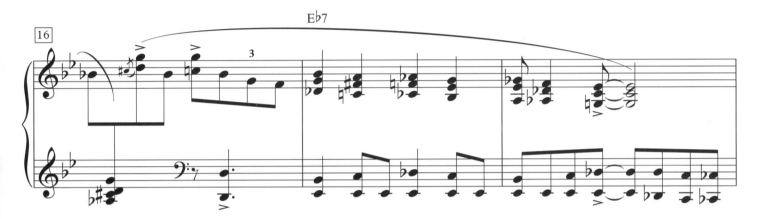

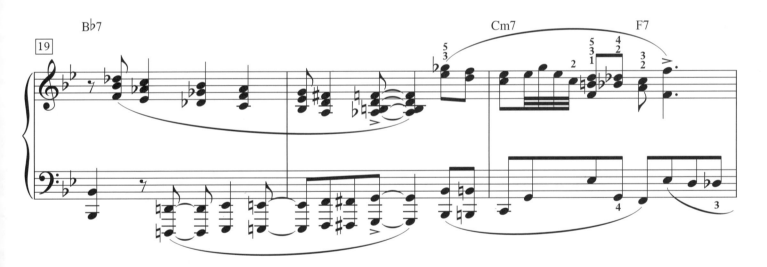

Postlude

Congratulations on completing your blues ABCs. As you can tell by now, the blues has become a vibrant musical form because innovative musicians have pushed the simple twelve-measure progression in new and exciting directions, combining the blues with new musical trends and contemporary styles. Your voice is needed to push the blues into the 21st century and beyond. Keep practicing, studying, and getting funky in your own unique way!

ALSO BY JEREMY SISKIND

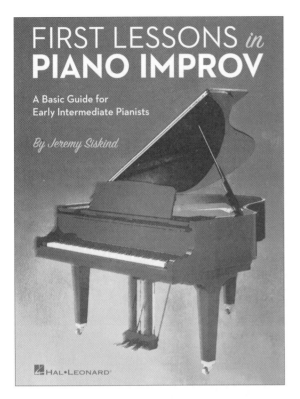

FIRST LESSONS IN PIANO IMPROV
HL00159521

JAZZ BAND PIANIST
HL00296925

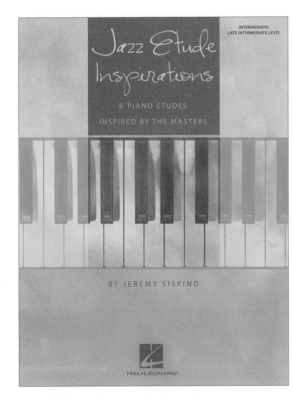

JAZZ ETUDE INSPIRATIONS
HL00296860

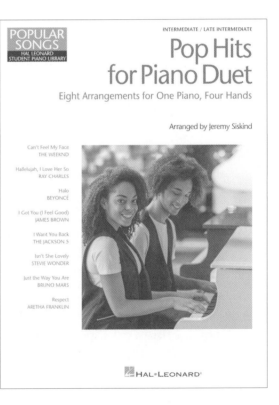

POP HITS FOR PIANO DUET
HL00224734

Available at **www.halleonard.com**.

About the Author

Pianist-composer **Jeremy Siskind** is "a genuine visionary" (*Indianapolis Star*) who "seems to defy all boundaries" (JazzInk) with music "rich in texture and nuance" (*Downbeat*).

A top finisher in several national and international jazz piano competitions, Siskind is a two-time laureate of the American Pianists Association and the winner of the Nottingham International Jazz Piano Competition. Since making his professional debut juxtaposing the Debussy *Etudes* with jazz standards at Carnegie Hall's Weill Hall, Siskind has established himself as one of the nation's most innovative and virtuosic modern pianists.

Siskind's multifaceted career often finds him combining musical styles and breaking aesthetic norms. As the leader of "The Housewarming Project," he has created "a shining example of chamber jazz" (*Downbeat*). He has also established himself as a pioneer of the in-home concert movement by presenting well over 100 house concerts in 26 states. In 2020, the Housewarming Project was a winner of a $30,000 grant from Chamber Music America's New Jazz Works program.

On the 2020 duo album, *Impressions of Debussy*, Siskind explores the Debussy preludes through improvisation with saxophonist Andrew Rathbun. Similarly, his 2019 book-CD project, *Perpetual Motion Etudes for Piano*, blurs the line between classical, through-composed piano etudes, and jazz-based improvisations, and invites other pianists to do the same through a self-published work that includes optional improvisation for each piece. Siskind has been experimenting with performing the pieces in collaboration with classical pianists, including Grammy-winner Angelin Chang, and through university residencies. Other projects include writing concert arrangements for soprano Julia Bullock and pianist-activist Lara Downes, composing the theme song for the 2017 Obie Awards, and serving as musical director for comediennes Lea DeLaria and Sandra Bernhard.

A highly-respected educator, Siskind has written 13 publications with Hal Leonard, including the landmark instructional books *Jazz Band Pianist* and *First Lessons in Piano Improv*. His self-published book *Playing Solo Jazz Piano* includes an introduction from jazz legend Fred Hersch, and is one of the top 50 best-selling jazz books on Amazon.com. He currently teaches at California's Fullerton College, chairs the National Conference for Keyboard Pedagogy's *Creativity Track*, and spreads peace through music in places like Lebanon, Tunisia, and Thailand with the non-profit organization Jazz Education Abroad.

Jeremy Siskind is a Yamaha artist.